Salt Block Cooking

Graham Hodson

Salt Block Cooking

© Graham Hodson 2020 All Rights Reserved

The moral right of the author has been asserted

First published by Rockwood Publishing 2020

Take a look at more great books available from
Rockwood Publishing

… **some for FREE!**

Just click the link below:

rockwoodpublishing.co.uk

Table of Contents

Himalayan Salt Blocks

The Himalayan Mountains stand at a site that was once a primordial sea, and within that ancient, primal body of water, there existed a perfect ecosystem.

The sea eventually evaporated under the intense heat of the sun and as it receded, it left behind its rich, life-giving minerals in the form of deep veins of salt.

Over millions of years, the earth's tectonic plates moved, and at the junction of the Indian and Eurasian plates, a grindingly slow, but nonetheless immensely powerful collision took place, which resulted in the mountain range of the Himalayas being born, as each tectonic plate pushed unforgivingly against the other, forcing the landmass to climb higher and higher into the air.

Himalayan salt, formed over 250,000,000 years ago and free from all pollutants, is now mined from deposits in the foothills of the Salt Range hill system at the Khewra Salt Mine in Jhelum, part of the Punjab region of Pakistan. It's the world's oldest and second-largest salt mine and attracts up to 275,000 visitors per year.

Known locally over hundreds of years for its preventative and restorative effect on the human body, it has been hand-mined and used by the people of the Himalaya region for centuries and is still a major part of their indigenous culture.

One of the most popular uses of Himalayan salt, due to its inherent stability and heat retention, is that of the salt block for cooking.

As previously stated, Himalayan salt was formed under the most intense pressure from the movement of tectonic plates, which means that as a substance, it is quite dense and so has very little space in which to absorb moisture.

This is why it can be carved, cut or sculptured into various shapes and why it can withstand extreme temperatures, hot or cold. It is what's termed a "stable" substance.

A positive outcome of its density, from the point of view of cooking, is how evenly heat radiates throughout the whole block, leading to a uniformity of cooking across the whole surface, and also how the block retains its heat for longer.

Cooking on Himalayan salt blocks, which can also be called "Salt Slabs" or "Cooking Blocks", is becoming more and more popular, not just amongst the "foodie" community, but also with everyday folk like you and me. At this point in the book, you will already understand the many health benefits that can be derived from Himalayan salts, and the use of a salt block is a very sensible, easy, and healthy way of deriving those benefits.

Although most people appreciate the positive impact upon health associated with the minerals and electrolytes found within Himalayan salt, they also, understandably, might feel a little concerned that cooking on a Himalayan salt block will make everything taste... well... salty (!) and that the taste of the salt will overpower the natural flavours of the food. This is definitely not the case because, as discussed, the salt block is extremely dense and, as such, only imparts a hint of salt flavouring into the food that is being cooked.

It is a very subtle enhancement and is in no way overpowering with many people commenting on how much better the food tastes in comparison to sprinkling the salt on the meal just prior to serving. This is largely due to the fact that the subtle flavor of the salt becomes an integral part of the dish during the cooking process, and the difference can be compared to that of cooking meat while in a sauce, as opposed to just pouring the sauce over the meat at the end.

The amount of salt that is absorbed into the food will depend on how hot the block is and on the inherent properties of the food being prepared, in particular, the water and oil content. Talking of oil, if you use oil during the cooking process – I'm a massive fan of organic extra virgin olive oil – then you must very lightly oil the food and not the block, as retained oil could go rancid or even catch fire next time you use the cooking block.

It's important that the salt block is heated slowly, with most manufacturers recommending an increase of no more than

90°C per 15 minutes, even though it's excellent for high-temperature cooking as it can be heated to just under 800°C, but a word of caution here:-

Because of its dense nature, and therefore ability to retain heat over a long period of time, it is always best to put the heated block straight onto a carrying rack once cooking is complete.

This can help stop unnecessary accidents because you will automatically carry the block with the handles of the rack, even after it's been left for a period of time, otherwise, you may not realize just how hot it still is and pick up the block directly.

NB Please be careful handling the block once it's hot, as the heat from it could easily come through conventional oven gloves.

Although it can take a while to heat up the salt block to the required temperature for cooking, it retains its heat for a few hours. So, for those who are considering the energy costs and any environmental issues, it works out better than conventional cooking because once the block is at an optimum temperature, the oven/hob can be turned off as opposed to keeping the appliance on throughout the cooking process.

So... salt blocks are good for the environment too!

Graham Hodson

Tempering/Curing a Brand-new Himalayan Salt Block

B efore you use your Himalayan Salt Block for the first time you must 'temper' it.

There are two popular ways of doing this, but please refer to individual manufacturer's instructions:

1) Put the block into a <u>cold</u> oven and set it to 250 degrees F (130 C). Doing this will ensure that the oven and the block heat up slowly together. Once the oven reaches 250 degrees, turn off the oven, remove the block and leave to stand for about ½ hour, and then repeat the process, being sure that the oven cools down in the meantime. Performing this process twice will ensure that the block is properly tempered. Your Himalayan salt block is now ready for use and can safely be heated up to 500 degrees, which is the recommended cooking temperature.

2) Place the block in the cold oven or on the hob (standing on a grill, of course, if it's an electric hob) and heat at a low temperature for 15 – 20 mins, then on medium heat for 15 – 20 mins, then on high heat for 15 – 20 mins.

Every time you use the block from here on in, it will take approx. 45 minutes in the oven/on the hob to reach the ideal cooking temperature.

Heating the block will sometimes change the surface appearance, and it may also crackle a little. This is nothing to be alarmed about and is all part of the curing/heating process.

To test if the salt block is hot enough for cooking, splatter a few drops of water on the surface and they should dance around and **evaporate** immediately. You must be careful not to touch it and always remember that it gets extremely hot and retains its heat for a very long time.

Some people test if the block is hot enough by carefully holding their hand 2 – 3 inches above the block, and if they can't keep it there for more than a few seconds, it's hot enough for use. I DON'T recommend doing this, but if you do elect to adopt this method, PLEASE be extremely careful not to burn yourself.

The salt blocks need to remain completely dry for 24 hours between uses.

The idea is to heat the oven while the slat block is already inside. This is usually a gentle enough increase in heat to keep the block from cracking, but PLEASE always refer to the manufacturer's specific instructions.

Also, please remember that different thicknesses of salt block will require different increments of temperature.

Bonuses associated with a Himalayan salt cooking block include: -

1. Being a naturally antibacterial and antimicrobial surface, it's easy to clean by simply using a damp sponge/cloth (with NO soap).

2. It can be used as a cold plate for salads and fruit.

3. They are very durable and, with proper care, can last a long time (it's usually a good idea to always use the same side of the block for cooking the food, as this has been shown to make the block last longer).

4. It looks amazing - and even if you don't use it to prepare a particular meal, it can be used as a serving platter.

Only purchase a salt block from a supplier who operates a guaranteed returns policy, because if they don't offer this facility, there's a pretty good chance that it's a fake.

Please always refer to the full manufacturer's instructions concerning the use and maintenance of the cooking block. This will ensure your safety and help you achieve the best results, and also give the longest life to your salt block.

Graham Hodson

Care for Your Salt Block

I t's important for the longevity of your salt block that you administer proper care. Here are a few tips:

- Heat the salt block slowly, increasing the temperature gradually over a period of time. This is especially important for the first few uses
- NEVER put the salt block in a dish-washer
- The block can be placed directly over a gas burner, but if you're using an electric hob, be sure to place the block on a grate or metal ring in order to create a flow of air around/under the salt block. Don't place it directly onto the heat source of an electric oven/hob
- NEVER pour oils onto the food while on the salt block
- Always be sure that the block is completely clean and dry prior to use
- Let the block cool naturally

- The block must be completely cool before cleaning
- NEVER use soap or cleaning products of any kind, only use a sponge/cloth and warm water
- ALWAYS refer to the individual manufacturer's cleaning instructions

And now, onto the main event... THE RECIPES!

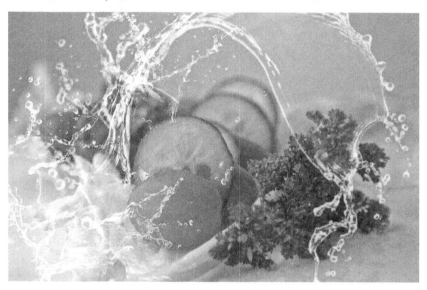

Recipes

Below are 12 mouthwatering, delicious, lip-smacking and yet easy to make recipes, one for each month of the year. However, if you get a taste for it – pun entirely intended! – why not make cooking on a Himalayan salt block a weekly event?

There are meat dishes, fish dishes, desserts, and snacks.

Where the recipe is for the main part of a meal, you can add your own accompaniments like potatoes, rice, pasta, bread, vegetables etc. to turn it into your own creation.

Obviously, if you wish you can add any sort of extras to your liking – pepper, garlic, olive oil, paprika, turmeric, balsamic vinegar, mint leaves, bay leaves, rocket, spinach etc. etc. either during the cooking process or afterwards, but you more than likely don't need to add salt as there is usually enough infused into the ingredients during their time on the salt plate.

Experiment and... **ENJOY!**

Beautiful Beef

Serves 4

Total prep and cooking time: 30 mins

Ingredients

- 1 ½ Tablespoons toasted sesame oil
- 1 ½ Tablespoons canola oil
- 1 ½ teaspoons minced garlic
- 2 teaspoons minced fresh ginger
- 2 Tablespoons sugar
- ¼ cup thinly sliced green onions
- 2 strip steaks, each about 10 oz. and 1 inch thick, thinly sliced
- ½ red onion, thinly sliced
- 1 large jalapeño (optional) thinly sliced

Directions

In a large bowl, whisk together the sesame oil, canola oil, garlic, ginger, sugar and green onions.

Add the beef, red onion (and optional jalapeño if desired) and toss until well mixed.

Stand at room temperature for approx. 30 minutes to marinade.

Place the beef on the Himalayan salt block (in single layers) and cook, turning once, until browned on both sides.

This should equate to approximately 1 to 2 minutes per side. Serve the beef immediately.

Mouth-watering!

Graham Hodson

Bonkers Bananas with Ice Cream and Cherries

Serves 4

This uses a cold/chilled Himalayan salt block/plate.

Ingredients

- 2 bananas
- Sugar and caramel
- 1 pint chocolate/vanilla/mint ice cream
- ¼ cup cherries (with juice)
- 4 slices roasted pineapple
- 4 oz whipped cream

Directions

Place the pineapple in an oven to warm through (approx. 10 minutes)

Peel and cut the bananas in half lengthwise, then cut in half across the banana and sprinkle with a little sugar.

Place the warmed pineapple on the Himalayan salt plate, and add the bananas on either side.

Add cherries and drizzle with cherry juice.

Place the ice cream of your choice on top of the pineapple, bananas, and cherries and drizzle with room temperature caramel.

Top with whipped cream and serve on the salt block.

Soooooooooooooooooooo good!

Graham Hodson

Himalayan Chicken

Serves: 4

Time to prepare and cook: approx. 45 mins

Ingredients

- 1 Tablespoon finely chopped rosemary
- 3 Tablespoons lemon juice
- 3 Tablespoons extra-virgin olive oil
- 1 teaspoon crushed red pepper
- 3/8 teaspoon coarse sea salt
- ¼ teaspoon ground black pepper
- 2 minced garlic cloves
- 4 x 6-ounce skinless, boneless chicken breast halves
- Lemon

Directions

Mix the first 7 ingredients listed above in a bowl to make a marinade. Put the chicken in the bowl and make sure that it is fully coated with the marinade.

Refrigerate for 20 minutes.

Remove chicken and discard any remaining marinade.

Place the chicken on the preheated Himalayan salt block and cook until chicken is done on both sides (always check that the chicken is thoroughly cooked through to the centre by cutting a piece of chicken in half and making sure that there is no pink meat visible).

18

Sprinkle with lemon juice and serve immediately with boiled potatoes and fresh seasonal vegetables.

Chocolate Chip Cookies (oh, yes!)

Yield: approx. 24 cookies

Ingredients

- 1¼ cups flour
- ½ teaspoon baking soda
- ¼ - ½ teaspoon salt
- ½ cup butter
- ½ cup brown sugar
- ¼ cup granulated sugar
- 1 large egg
- ¾ teaspoon vanilla extract
- 1¼ cups chocolate chunks

Directions

Stir the flour, baking soda and salt together and set to one side.

Cream the butter and sugars together for about 2-3 minutes.

Add the egg and vanilla and beat until well combined.

Slowly add all the dry ingredients until completely blended.

Stir in the chocolate chunks.

Place rounded spoonfuls onto the salt block, spacing each cookie a few inches apart, and bake for about 10-12 minutes.

Let them sit for at least 5 minutes before placing them on a cooling rack.

Repeat this procedure until all of the batter is used.

Graham Hodson

Made in minutes... devoured in seconds!

Scrumptious Baked Salmon

Ingredients

- 8 tablespoons of extra virgin olive oil
- ¼ cup of parsley
- ¼ cup fresh basil
- juice of 1 lemon
- 2 cloves of garlic
- 1 teaspoon black pepper
- 1 ½ pounds of salmon, cut into two pieces
- 8 baby tomatoes
- 3 shallots, cut into halves
- 2 stems of fresh rosemary
- ¼ cup Parmesan cheese
- 1 bunch of asparagus

Directions

Prepare the marinade with six tablespoons of olive oil, parsley, basil, lemon juice, garlic, one shallot, and black pepper.

Put the mixture in a glass bowl with the salmon, cover and marinate in the refrigerator for about an hour.

Preheat the oven to 400 degrees F (200 degrees C) with the Himalayan salt block in the oven so that it heats slowly.

Place the two shallots, asparagus, and red tomatoes in a baking dish and brush with two tablespoons of olive oil, Parmesan, and a little pepper.

Put into the oven for 20–30 minutes.

Place the fish and rosemary on the pre-heated salt block and cook for 7–10 min on each side.

Delicious!

Skewered Tomatoes and Cheese Balls

Serves 4

Total prep and cooking time: 10 minutes to prepare, but 3 hours left in the fridge

This is a little bit different and shows the versatility of a Himalayan salt block. This time we're not using it to cook with, but instead using it as a prep board and serving platter. During its 3 hours or so in the fridge, the block will impart a wonderful, slightly salty flavour to the food, and then you serve it up straight from the fridge while the food is still on the salt block! Fab! ☺

Ingredients

- 12 cherry tomatoes, halved
- 12 bocconcini (mozzarella cheese balls)
- 12 small basil leaves
- Extra-virgin olive oil
- Freshly ground pepper (optional)

Directions

In order, put half a tomato,1 bocconcini, 1 basil leaf and the other half of the tomato onto a small skewer.

Lightly drizzle with olive oil and season with pepper (if desired)

Place on a Himalayan salt block.

Transfer to the refrigerator for 3 hours, turning the skewers over after about 1 1/2 hours to ensure even absorption of the salt from the block into the food.

Just serve directly from the fridge on the salt block/plate.

24

Graham Hodson

The most delicious little party nibble... EVER!

Chopped Beef on a Salt Plate

Serves 6

Total time: 15 mins prep time, then 30 – 60 mins in the fridge

With this dish, you are using the salt block for both infusing the food with flavour <u>and</u> as a serving dish!

<u>Ingredients</u>

- 12 oz. Pre-cooked beef cut into very small dice
- 1 Tablespoon extra-virgin olive oil
- 1 ½ Tablespoons finely chopped shallot
- 1 ½ Tablespoons chopped parsley
- ¼ cup capers, drained and roughly chopped
- 1 teaspoon Worcestershire sauce
- 2 or 3 dashes of a hot sauce (optional)
- 1 egg yolk
- Freshly cracked pepper
- Garlic French bread

<u>Directions</u>

Place the beef in a bowl, drizzle with olive oil and stir well.

Add the shallot, parsley, capers, egg yolk, Worcestershire and (optional) hot sauce.

Stir the ingredients until they are well mixed and season with pepper.

Transfer the whole mixture to the pre-chilled salt plate, forming a 1/2- to 3/4-inch layer.

Put the salt plate in the refrigerator for 30 - 60 minutes to allow the salt to flavour the dish.

Serve with warm, garlic French bread.

Mmmmmmmmm!

Luscious Lamb with Garlic Potatoes

Serves 2 people

Ingredients

- 4 lamb loin chops
- 1 Tablespoon oregano
- ½ teaspoon cumin
- ½ teaspoon coriander
- 4 cloves minced garlic
- 1 lb. red potatoes
- 1 teaspoon smoked paprika
- ½ teaspoon black pepper
- 2 Tablespoon extra virgin olive oil

Directions

Cut potatoes into quarters and brush with olive oil, then sprinkle them with smoked paprika, black pepper and minced garlic.

Place potatoes in roasting pan and cook.

Mix cumin, coriander, and oregano, and then rub the lamb chops with the mixture.

Brush the coated lamb chops with olive oil and place them onto the pre-heated Himalayan salt plate.

Cook for 4-6 minutes on each side until cooked to your liking.

Serve with the garlic roast potatoes and seasonal vegetables.

Feel those taste buds explode!

Graham Hodson

Super Scallop Fragilistic

Serves 4

Ingredients

For the Glaze:

- 2 tablespoons organic butter
- 1 small shallot, finely minced
- 1 medium garlic clove, finely minced
- 3 tablespoons of honey
- 2 tablespoons of fresh lemon juice
- 1½ teaspoons of black pepper

For the Vinaigrette:

- 1 teaspoon Dijon mustard
- 1 tablespoon sherry vinegar
- ¼ cup extra-virgin olive oil
- ½ pint cherry tomatoes (cut in ½)
- 1 tablespoon sliced basil leaves
- 1 pound large sea scallops (abductor muscle removed)

Directions

Honey cracked pepper glaze:

Melt the butter in a small saucepan over medium heat.

Add shallots and garlic and cook until shallots have softened (about 3 to 4 minutes).

Add honey, lemon juice and black pepper.

Stir well and season with salt and pepper.

Vinaigrette:

Whisk to combine the mustard and vinegar in a small bowl.

Slowly add the olive oil into the mixture until well combined.

Stir in the cherry tomatoes.

Season with salt and pepper.

Cook the scallops:

Brush the scallops with the glaze mixture.

Place scallops directly on the salt block and cook until lightly browned (about 2 to 3 minutes).

Turn scallops onto a clean spot on the block, brush again with the glaze and continue cooking until the centre is slightly opaque, which normally takes about 2 to 3 minutes more.

To serve:

Drizzle 2 to 3 tablespoons of vinaigrette over the scallops and serve immediately.

Utterly gorgeous!

Sea Bass Delight

Serves 2

Total prep and cooking time: 20 mins

Ingredients

- 2 Sea Bass Fillets
- Almond oil or Extra Virgin Olive Oil
- 1 bunch broccolini
- Lemon halves (for garnish)

Directions

Prepare the broccolini (which is similar to broccoli) by boiling in a large pan of salted water for approximately 1 minute.

Drain, and then dry on paper towels.

Brush a small amount of almond oil/olive oil on both sides of the sea bass fillets.

Place the sea bass fillets on the heated salt block along with the broccolini. They must be put on separate parts of the salt block, **NOT** on top of one another.

Brown the sea bass lightly on both sides.

The broccolini should turn a brilliant green. You'll know when the broccolini is done when you can insert a sharp knife point into it without much resistance.

The sea bass will be done in minutes and can be tested by "pulling" at the middle of the fish with a fork, and it should just "flake" fairly easily.

Graham Hodson

A mouth-watering and healthy meal in minutes!

NB If you prefer, you can use halibut instead of sea bass.

Spicy Skewered Vegetables

Serves 6 – 8

Total time (prep and cooking) 45 mins

Ingredients

- 2 jars (each 12 oz.) artichoke hearts
- 1 bunch asparagus, ends trimmed, spears cut into 3-inch pieces
- 1 red onion, cut into slices 1 inch thick
- 1 lb. halloumi cheese, cut into 2-inch cubes
- 2 to 3 Tbs. spicy potlatch seasoning
- Extra-virgin olive oil

Directions

In a large bowl, combine the artichoke hearts, asparagus, onion and cheese.

Sprinkle with the potlatch seasoning and mix thoroughly.

Put the vegetables and cheese onto skewers (alternating with each other) spacing them evenly.

Brush olive oil onto the cheese and vegetables.

Working in batches, place the skewers on the salt plate and cook, turning once, until the vegetables are tender and the cheese is browned. This usually takes about 4 minutes per side.

Serve immediately.

Deeeeeeeeeelicious!

Graham Hodson

Simply Splendid Shrimps

Serves: 4

Ingredients

- 2 tablespoons unsalted butter
- 1 small shallot, peeled and finely minced
- 1 medium garlic clove, peeled and finely minced
- 3 tablespoons of pure honey
- 2 tablespoons fresh lemon juice
- 1½ teaspoons cracked black pepper
- 1 pound large shrimp

Directions

Honey cracked pepper glaze:

Melt the butter over medium heat in a small saucepan.

Add shallots and garlic and cook until shallots have softened – this usually takes about 3 to 4 minutes.

Add the honey, lemon juice and black pepper.

Stir and season with salt and pepper.

Cook the shrimp:

Brush the shrimp with the glaze mixture.

Place shrimp directly on the salt block and cook until lightly browned (about 2 to 3 minutes).

Turn the shrimp onto a clean place on the Himalayan salt block.

Re-brush with glaze and continue cooking until the center is slightly opaque, about 2 to 3 minutes more.

To serve:

Drizzle with 2 to 3 tablespoons of the glaze mixture and serve immediately.

BONUS IDEAS

Thin-Cut Steak

A Himalayan salt block is *brilliant* for cooking thinly cut steak!

If you cut the meat into 2 – 3 inch lengths, but only ¼ inch in thickness, then once the salt block is up to full heat, you simply place the strips of beef onto the block for no more than 10 seconds (YES – seconds!!) on each side and the meat will be beautifully cooked and ready to serve, for example, on a bun with any extras of your choosing, or with new/boiled potatoes and seasonal vegetables for a very quick and very healthy meal.

Just as with any kind of grilling/barbecuing, cook the meat for as little or as long as you wish, but keep turning it regularly so as not to scorch the meat (there are lots of reports saying that burnt meat is *not at all* good for you!)

Some people like to toss the thin cuts of beef in olive oil and/or black pepper prior to cooking. This is a great idea if you wish, but remember NOT to add salt as there will be enough salt naturally infused into the meat from the salt block during the cooking process.

Bacon and Eggs

A Himalayan salt block isn't just for the fancy stuff! Many salt block owners use it to cook simple things… like bacon and egg!

Simply cook the bacon on both sides, being careful not to overdo it as they cook really quite quickly, while at the same time cracking an egg onto the surface of the block.

The egg white initially runs to the edges, but because it's so hot it is more often than not stopped in its tracks by the heat from the block (it doesn't matter if any of the egg white makes it to the edge as it can be quickly and simply cleaned off with a sponge and warm water later).

Some like to toss the bacon in olive oil prior to cooking, and some like to put the egg _directly on top_ of the bacon during the cooking process. It's all good! ☺

Tenderloin Steak

Tenderloin steak, if cut to 1-inch thickness, only takes about 2 – 3 minutes cooking on each side.

Once cooked, you can then slice the steak and drizzle with olive oil and season with black pepper, but remember – DON'T ADD SALT! ☺

So, there you go!

I sincerely hope that you liked the recipe ideas and that you thoroughly enjoy making, eating, and maybe even sharing your fabulous food… treating yourself and others to a truly wonderful, special meal!

Thank you for reading, and I wish you health and happiness wherever you may go.

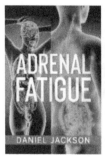

Take a look at more great books available from
Rockwood Publishing

… **some for FREE!**

Just click the link below:

rockwoodpublishing.co.uk

no responsibility for, and will not be liable for, the websites being temporarily unavailable or being removed from the Internet. The accuracy and completeness of the information provided herein and opinions stated herein are not guaranteed or warranted to produce any particular results, and the advice and strategies contained herein may not be suitable for every individual. The author shall not be liable for any loss incurred as a consequence of the use and application, directly or indirectly, of any information presented in this work. This publication is designed to provide information in regards to the subject matter covered. The information included in this book has been compiled to give an overview of the subject(s) and detail some of the symptoms, treatments etc. that are available to people with this condition. It is not intended to give medical advice. For a firm diagnosis of your condition, and for a treatment plan suitable for you, you should consult your doctor or consultant. The writer of this book and the publisher are not responsible for any damages or negative consequences following any of the treatments or methods highlighted in this book. Website links are for informational purposes and should not be seen as a personal endorsement; the same applies to the products detailed in this book. The reader should also be aware that although the web links included were correct at the time of writing, they may become out of date in the future.

Disclaimers

The content contained within this book is for information and entertainment purposes only, and in no way purports to represent professional medical opinion. It should NOT be used as a substitute for expert advice, and you must consult with your designated health professional before acting upon any information contained herein or before undertaking any practice whose methodology is referred to in this book. The author is NOT a registered health professional and the text merely represents personal opinion, not medical fact. The author cannot be held responsible for the consequences of any action derived from the reading of this book, as the content is not based on diagnosis and subsequent regimen. It is the reader's responsibility to seek proper, professional medical advice from a registered health practitioner in connection with any material contained within this book.

Legal Disclaimer (part 1)

Nothing in this book should be construed as an attempt to diagnose, treat or cure. The information in this book is intended to be a community resource. The author takes no responsibility for any informational material or brochures produced using information taken from this book. The author has endeavoured to ensure that all information is correct at the time of publication. This information, however, is subject to change without notice. The author makes no warranty concerning the accuracy of any information and will not be liable for any errors or omissions. Any liability that arises as a result of this information is hereby excluded to the fullest extent allowed by law.

This information should not be used as a substitute for seeking independent professional advice.

Legal Disclaimer (part 2)

Disclaimer and Terms of Use:

indirect, or punitive damages as well as any circumstance for any complication, injuries, side effects or other medical accidents to person or property arising from or in connection with the use or reliance upon any information contained herein.

e) The author is not responsible for the contents of any linked site or any link contained in a linked site, or any changes or update to such sites. The inclusion of any link does not imply endorsement by the author. The author makes no representations or claims as to the quality, content and accuracy of the information, services, products, messages which may be provided by such resources, and specifically disclaims any warranties, including but not limited to implied or express warranties of merchantability or fitness for any particular usage, application or purpose.

f) The information provided is general in nature and is intended for educational and informational purposes only. It is not intended to replace or substitute the evaluation, judgment, diagnosis, and medical or preventative care of a physician, paediatrician, therapist and/or health care provider.

g) Any medical, nutritional, dietetic, therapeutic or other decisions, dosages, treatments or drug regimes should be made in consultation with a health care practitioner. Do not discontinue treatment or medication without first consulting your physician, clinician or therapist.

h) By reading this information, you signify your assent to these terms and conditions of use. If you do not agree to these terms and conditions of use, do not read/use this information. If any provision of these terms and conditions of use shall be determined to be unlawful, void or for any reason unenforceable, then that provision shall be deemed severable from this agreement and shall not affect the validity and enforceability of any remaining provisions.

i) The information, services, products, messages and other materials, individually and collectively, are provided with the understanding that the author is not engaged in rendering medical advice or recommendations.

j) The information and the terms of use are subject to change without notice. The material provided as is without warranty of any kind and may include inaccuracies and/or typographical errors. The author makes no representations about the suitability of this information for any purpose. The author disclaims all warranties with regard to this information, including all implied warranties, and in no event shall the author be held liable, resulting from, or in any way related to, the use of this information.

k) The unauthorized alteration of the content of this information is expressly prohibited. The author, its agents and representatives shall not be responsible for any claims, actions or damages which may arise on account of the unauthorized alteration of this information.

Made in the USA
Monee, IL
10 June 2023

35578267R00031